From the desktop of Jeffrey Simmons

A vacation in Paris inspired Miroslav Sasek to create childrens travel guides to the big cities of the world. He brought me *This is Paris* in 1958 when I was publishing in London, and we soon followed up with *This is London*. Both books were enormously successful, and his simple vision grew to include more than a dozen books. Their amusing verse, coupled with bright and charming illustrations, made for a series unlike any other, and garnered Sasek (as we always called him) the international and popular acclaim he deserved.

I was thrilled to learn that *This is London* will once again find its rightful place on bookshelves. Sasek is no longer with us (and I have lost all contact with his family), but I am sure he would be delighted to know that a whole new generation of wide-eyed readers is being introduced to his whimsical, imaginative, and enchanting world.

Your name here

Published by arrangement with Simon & Schuster Books for Young Readers,
Simon & Schuster Children's Publishing Division

This edition first published in 2004 by
UNIVERSE PUBLISHING
A Division of Rizzoli International Publications, Inc.
300 Park Avenue South
New York, NY 10010
www.rizzoliusa.com

*See updated London facts at end of book

2012 2013 / 22 21 20

Printed in China

ISBN-13: 978-0-7893-1062-0

Library of Congress Catalog Control Number: 2003114669

Cover design: centerpointdesign
Universe editor: Jane Ginsberg

M. Sasek

This is LONDON

UNIVERSE

Well, this is London.

But don't worry, it is hidden in fog like this only a few times a year in winter. Most of the time it looks —

like this!

London is the capital of the United Kingdom and
the chief city of the British Commonwealth of Nations.
It is the largest city in the world.*

"Busy emporium for trade and traders," it was
described by the Roman historian, Tacitus, one
thousand nine hundred years ago.

There are ten thousand streets in London. When in doubt about how to get to one of them, ask a policeman.

This one belongs to the Metropolitan Police.

This one is from the City.

The City is in the heart of London.

The City begins right at the Temple Bar Memorial.

The City of London, the London of Roman times, is the "centre" around which the great capital city has grown.

In the heart of the City is the Bank of England. "The Old Lady of Threadneedle Street" is the most important bank in the country. The building on the right is the Royal Exchange.

The City of London has only six thousand inhabitants,
but hundreds of thousands work here during the day.

Here they are arriving on Monday —

and here they are at home on Sunday.

This is St. Paul's Cathedral, built 1675 – 1710 by Christopher Wren.

Inside you can find the tombs of Lord Nelson, the Duke of Wellington, and other great men of England's great past.

Christopher Wren, too, is buried here. On his tomb you read this inscription: "If you seek my monument, look around."

One of the smallest, and one of the oldest churches in London is St. Ethelburga.*

Here is The Monument, designed by Wren to commemorate the Great Fire of London in 1666 which destroyed most of the old city.

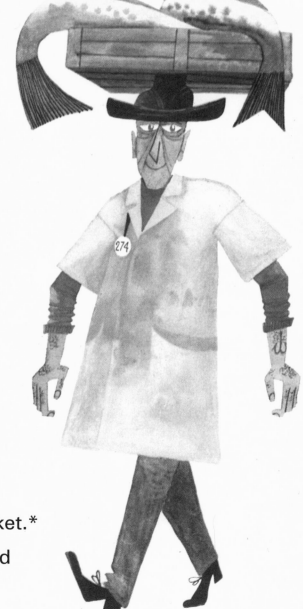

Nearby is the Billingsgate fish market.* Look at the hat, made of leather and wood to carry the heaviest fish.

Fleet Street looks like this from
the top of a bus. It is here that
newspapers are made.*

This is one of some six thousand buses in London.

There is green countryside all around London. You can get there on a Green Line coach.

You may have to join a bus queue —

Queuing is for a Londoner a kind of sport. Entertaining a queue is for some a way to make a living.

— or a queue of one's own.

This is Piccadilly Circus at night.

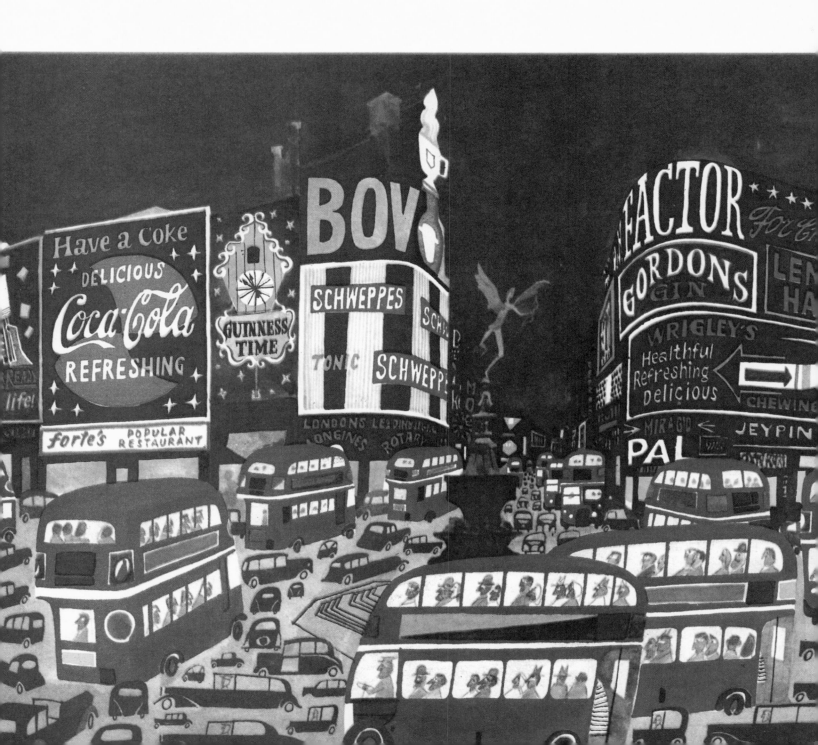

The famous Drury Lane Theatre —

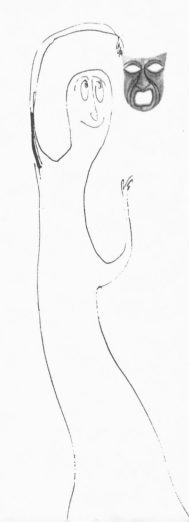

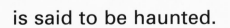

is said to be haunted.

Nearby is the actor's church, called
St. Paul's, like the cathedral. Around
it you will find Covent Garden market.*

"Taxi! Taxi!"

This is where since 1765
the best bowler hats have
been made.

"L" means that the driver is learning to drive.

St. James Palace, built by Henry VIII, used to be
the London residence of English kings and queens.

Today the Queen lives in
Buckingham Palace.

Outside the palace you see
bearskins. Under the bearskins are Guardsmen. To
recognize their regiments,
look at their plumes.

The Coldstreams

The Grenadiers

The Irish Guards

The Welsh Guards

The Scots Guards have no plume at all.

You will find there are many Guards in London.

This is the entrance in Whitehall to
Horse Guards' Parade. The Guards are
the Life Guards.

In Trafalgar Square you see Nelson's Column, the National
Gallery, peanut vendors, pigeons, and people.

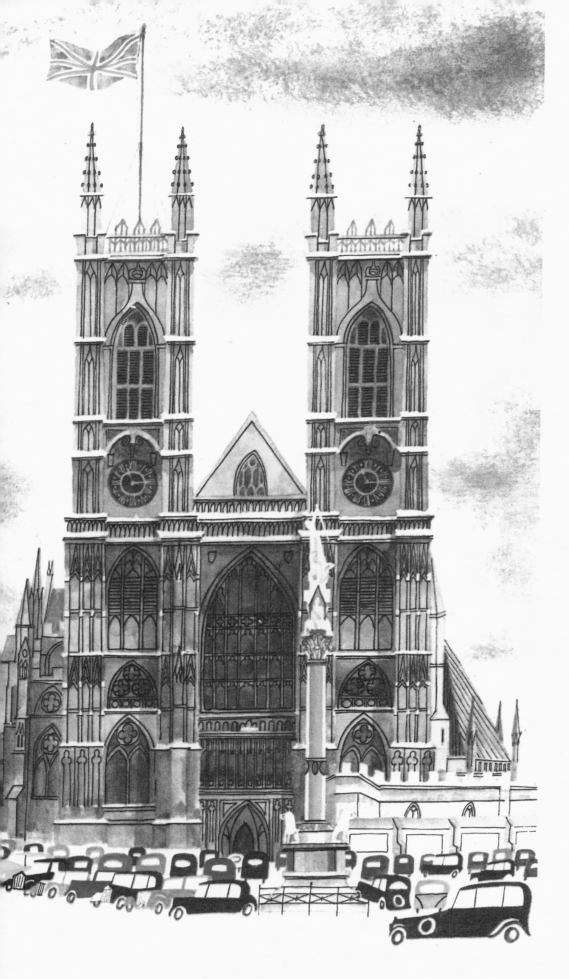

Westminster Abbey has watched the coronations of England's rulers
from William the Conqueror in 1066 to Elizabeth II in 1953.
Many of Britain's most famous men are buried there.

Lambeth Palace has been the London residence of the Archbishops of Canterbury for more than seven centuries.

Here is another official residence, 10 Downing Street, where British Prime Ministers live.

The Houses of Parliament stand on the site of the old Royal Palace of Westminster. The building contains eleven courtyards, a hundred staircases, a thousand rooms and about two miles of passages.

On the left is the Victoria Tower. When the House of Commons is sitting, a Union Jack flies from its top by day —

by night a light is shown on the Clock Tower.

The hours are struck by the famous bell "Big Ben"
and the minutes are shown by hands fourteen feet long.

This is one of the piers on the Thames from which you take a boat up or down the river.

Tower Bridge is the last bridge before you get to
the sea fifty miles away.* Here the London Docks begin.

Thousands of ships leave the Port of London each year
for "harbours" all over the world.

This is Her Majesty's Royal Fortress and Palace of the Tower of London.

Its central keep, the White Tower, was built by William the Conqueror in 1078. The Tower of London was used as a fortress, a royal palace, and a prison. Within its walls the blood of many illustrious prisoners was shed.

All school children love
to visit the Tower.

Here for centuries have been the Beefeaters
— or Yeomen Warders of the Tower —

and the ravens.

The address of this ship is Victoria Embankment, London.
It is H. M. S. Discovery, the famous polar research ship
of Captain Scott.*

Five miles down the river,
Meridian Zero passes through
Greenwich. The Greenwich
Meridian measures the earth's
longitude and the world's time.

Speaking of time, London's tea-time is about four, but there is always
time for a cup of tea —

at a Lyons, perhaps.*

Milk may be brought to the door by the milkman.

When tea-time descends on London, it descends also on the parks.

Here you can sit on the grass —

see the statue of
Peter Pan in
Kensington Gardens —

meet a Nanny pushing a pram —

or listen to the speakers in
Hyde Park.

And since we have been above ground long enough, let us take a look under ground — at the Underground.

The platform

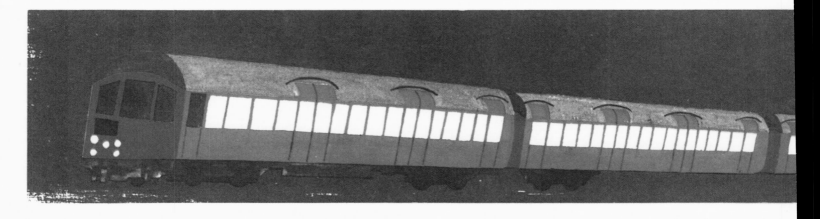

The train

Some three million passengers are carried daily in Underground trains.

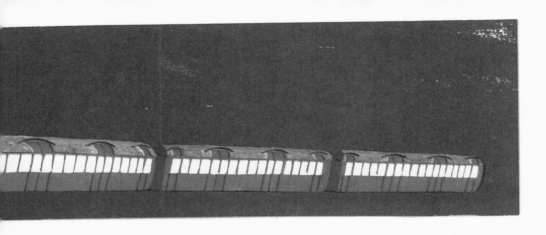

Don't forget to keep your ticket.

You must surrender it at the exit.*

In the middle of Grosvenor Square is the Roosevelt Memorial. The square is Little America in London.

Among the remains of old London is this famous old shop —

and these Elizabethan houses in High Holborn.

The best way to see London is from the top of a bus, but this is the way to see the Zoo.

If you are a cricket fan,
you may like to go to Lord's.

London is full of interest.

On Sunday morning you can go to Petticoat Lane
open-air market.

Charles II founded Chelsea Hospital, another famous building by Christopher Wren. It is a home for Britain's old soldiers.

Here is one of them —
a Chelsea Pensioner.

In Chelsea in May, there is a famous flower show.

If you like to climb up among the branches of trees —
try Battersea Park.

If you like flowers — try lavender, a traditional English scent.

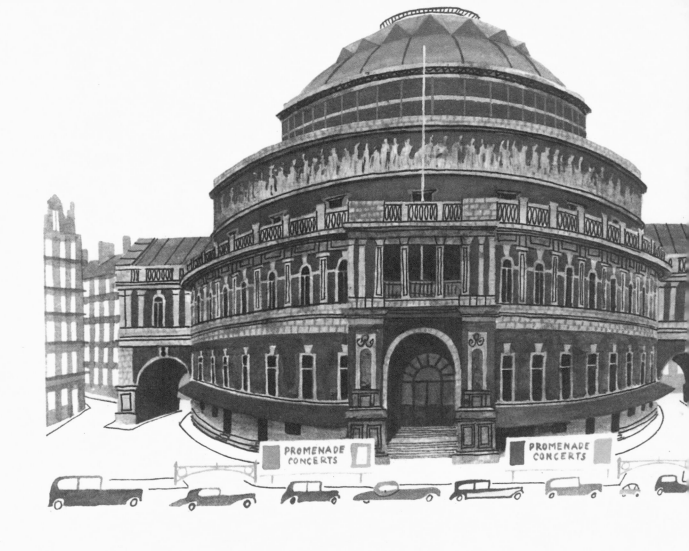

If you like music — try the Royal
Albert Hall.

Let's have a look at London's museums.

Here is Puffing Billy, the oldest steam-engine in the world, date 1813 —

and this is an exact copy of the "aeroplane" in which the Wright brothers made their first flight in 1903. Both are found in the Science Museum.

you will see Egyptian mummies four thousand years old.

There are many Mr. Smiths in London. One of
them sells books and has many shops and bookstalls,
like this one at Waterloo Station.

There are many department stores. The biggest is Selfridges.*

Neither the West African visitor nor this Scotsman is buying trousers!

In the big, busy capital are tiny, quiet streets called mews. Once these houses used to be stables.

Children are not allowed inside a pub.

But peep in and see what's going on.

The grown-ups are playing darts.

This pub, the Cheshire Cheese, is one of the oldest.

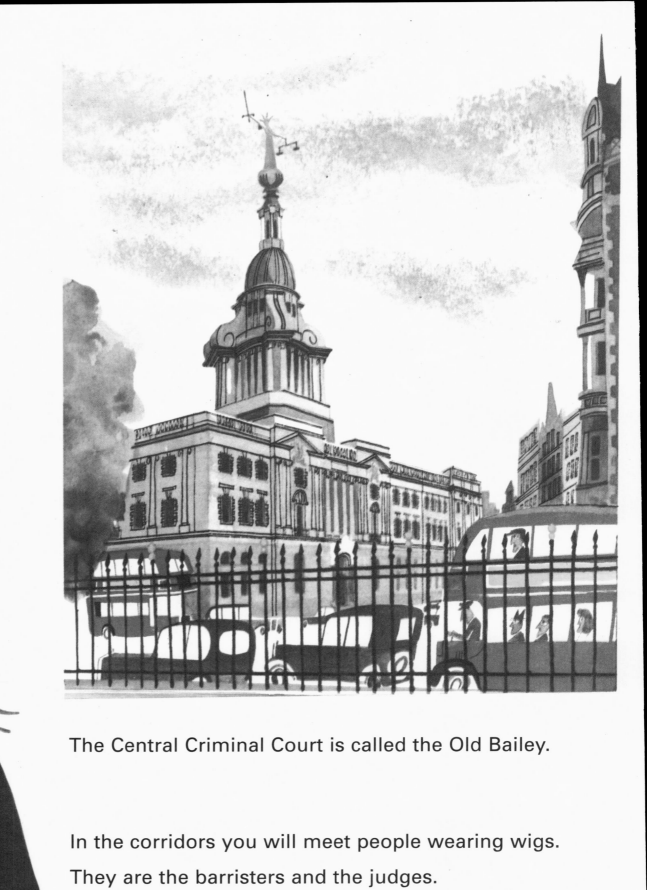

The Central Criminal Court is called the Old Bailey.

In the corridors you will meet people wearing wigs.
They are the barristers and the judges.

From the Old Bailey we go to New Scotland Yard.* The people the detectives catch go the other way.

This is a street-cleaner.
At the end of all things comes the broom.

And at the end of your picture of London there should come a mention for that faithful friend, your umbrella!

Because

this is London!